Science In Your Life:
FORCES
The Ups and Downs

Wendy Sadler

www.raintreepublishers.co.uk

Visit our website to find out more information about **Raintree** books.

To order:
☎ Phone 44 (0) 1865 888112
▤ Send a fax to 44 (0) 1865 314091
▥ Visit the Raintree bookshop at **www.raintreepublishers.co.uk** to browse our catalogue and order online.

First published in Great Britain by Raintree, Halley Court, Jordan Hill, Oxford OX2 8EJ, part of Harcourt Education.
Raintree is a registered trademark of Harcourt Education Ltd.

Editorial: Melanie Copland, Kate Buckingham, and Lucy Beevor
Design: Victoria Bevan
and Bridge Creative Services Ltd
Picture Research: Hannah Taylor
and Catherine Bevan
Production: Duncan Gilbert

Originated by Chroma Graphics (Overseas) Pte. Ltd
Printed and bound in China by
South China Printing Company

ISBN 1 844 43659 4
10 09 08 07 06
10 9 8 7 6 5 4 3 2 1

British Library Cataloguing in Publication Data
Sadler, Wendy
Forces. – (Science in your life)
531.6
A full catalogue record for this book is available from the British Library.

Acknowledgements
Alamy Images pp. 13 (David Wall), 8 (GPI Stock); BananaStock p. 5; Corbis pp. 12 (Jose Luis Pelaez, Inc), 4 (Gilbert Iundt; TempSport), 11 (Jim Arbogast), 19 (NASA/Roger Ressmeyer), 16 (Reuters/David Gray), 9 (Steve Raymer); Corbis Royalty Free pp. 6, 21; Getty Images p. 14 (Photodisc); Harcourt Education Ltd pp. 7t, 7b, 10, 17, 20, 22, 25, 26, 29 (Tudor Photography); Photographers Direct pp. 15 (Skip Dean), 23 (Transparencies, Inc), 24 (Chris Miles).

Cover photograph of boy sliding down water slide reproduced with permission of Corbis/Kelly-Mooney Photography.

Every effort has been made to contact copyright holders of any material reproduced in this book. Any omissions will be rectified in subsequent printings if notice is given to the publishers.

The paper used to print this book comes from sustainable resources.

Disclaimer
All the Internet addresses (URLs) given in this book were valid at the time of going to press. However, due to the dynamic nature of the Internet, some addresses may have changed, or sites may have changed or ceased to exist since publication. While the author and publishers regret any inconvenience this may cause readers, no responsibility for any such changes can be accepted by either the author or the publishers.

An adult should supervise all of the activities in this book.

Contents

Any words appearing in the text in bold, **like this**, are explained in the glossary.

Forces all around you

Forces are all around you! Whenever you push or pull something you are using a force. Forces can also make things start, stop, stretch, bend, and break.

To jump up into the air, you first push down on the ground with a force. The ground pushes you back up into the air!

High jumpers use forces to win gold medals.

Forces everywhere

A tennis racket or baseball bat makes a ball move by pushing it with a force. We say that the racket or bat **exerts** a force on the ball.

Your breath even exerts a force on a balloon when you are blowing it up!

The force of your breath blows the balloon up.

Pushing off

When you push something it always pushes you back. Sometimes you can feel the push and sometimes you cannot.

When you walk along the street you push down with your feet. The ground pushes up against your feet. You might not notice it, but if it did not push you back you would not be able to walk around!

The gas coming out of a rocket when it takes off pushes downwards and the rocket is forced upwards.

Forces in your life!

Blow up a balloon and then let it go. The balloon shoots off into the air! This is because forces come in pairs. The air gets pushed out of the balloon in one direction. The opposite force pushes the balloon in the other direction.

air pushes out here

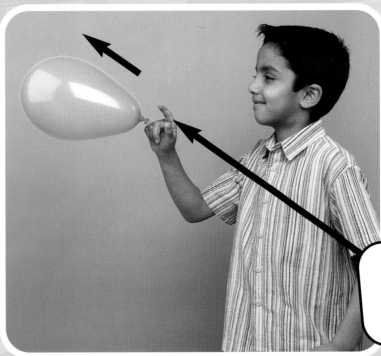

opposite force pushes the balloon forwards

Getting up to speed

Forces are used to get things moving or to stop things moving. Forces are also used to make things speed up, slow down, or change direction.

If an object is heavy it needs a big force to move it, stop it, or make it change direction. If you have ever tried to push an adult on a roundabout you will know that it is very difficult! It is much easier to push your friends on a roundabout because they **weigh** less than an adult and you need less force to move them.

When footballers head a ball, they push the ball with their head to make it go off in a different direction.

Heavy things need a big force to make them stop. You could easily stop an empty skateboard rolling towards you. But if you tried to stop a person on a skateboard you could get hurt. This is because the person and the skateboard together make a larger force.

Heavy things are hard to get moving. These tugs are using a pulling force to help the heavy tanker as it starts to move.

What is friction?

When one thing rubs against another there is a force between them. This force tries to slow the movement down.

The force that you get when two things rub together is called **friction**. This force can slow things down or even make them stop moving.

Friction can make things heat up. You can use friction to warm up your hands.

Some **materials**, such as rubber, make a lot of friction when you rub them together. This is because they have a rough or sticky surface. When things are very smooth and slippery there is not much friction. Ice is smooth and when you slide on it there is not much friction to slow you down.

Friction is useful for slowing things down. The brakes on a bike push against the wheel. This makes a lot of friction, which slows the wheels down.

Friction helps this extreme rock climber to grip on to the rock.

What would happen without friction?

If there was no friction between the laces of your shoes they would keep slipping undone and your shoes would fall off!

Slippery stuff

Sometimes there is not enough **friction** and this can cause problems. When roads are wet, the water stops car tyres from **gripping** properly. The water means there is less friction, so the car can **skid** more easily.

If you try to pick up a wet bar of soap you might find it is too slippery! There is only a very small amount of friction between your hand and the soap.

It is very hard to grip wet soap with your hands!

Having less friction can be fun, too. Water slides are faster than playground slides. The water makes the slide more slippery so there is less friction and you go faster.

If you try to go down a grass hill on a sledge you will not go very far or very fast. You need snow on the grass to make the friction less. You can travel faster down the hill when there is less friction.

Snow on the grass makes it slippery enough to sledge on.

Too much friction

Having too much **friction** can be a problem! When you try to pull something along the ground, it rubs against the ground. The friction force pulls in the opposite direction to the way you are trying to move. This makes it hard work!

Putting wheels on the bottom of an object helps to make the friction less, so it is easier to pull.

Inside a car engine there are lots of parts that move against each other very quickly. Lots of friction can make things hot, which could be dangerous inside an engine. Oil is used to make all the engine parts slippery. This means there is less friction so the engine does not get too hot.

Sometimes lids on jars can be hard to get undone. This is because there is too much friction between the lid and the jar.

Slowing down

Drag is another force that can affect objects that are moving. Drag can slow things down or make it difficult to get them moving in the first place. Drag is a force that pushes against objects moving in air or a liquid.

When you swim through the water in a swimming pool you can feel the water pushing against you. This drag force pushes against you when you are trying to move, and it slows you down.

Special suits made of very smooth material can help swimmers move faster through the water.

Making use of drag

When an aeroplane needs to slow down it uses drag. It puts up flaps on the wings so there is much more air pushing against the plane. The force of the air pushing against the plane helps slow it down so it can land safely.

Heavy stuff

Gravity is the name of the force that pulls everything towards the centre of Earth. Gravity makes it feel like we are all stuck to Earth's **surface**!

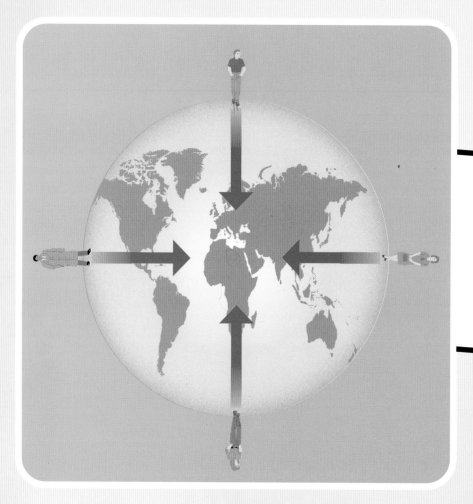

Gravity is a force that affects everyone all over the world. It pulls us all towards the centre of Earth.

What would happen without gravity?

Without gravity we would float in the air above the ground. This would make it very difficult to do most things!

Gravity is what makes things feel heavy. The **weight** of an object depends on how much of it there is. This is called its **mass**.

When a space rocket is a long way from Earth, there is no gravity pulling on it. The astronauts inside the rocket also do not feel any gravity pulling them down so they can float in the air!

Imagine what life would be like without gravity. Even standing up could be difficult!

Floating

If you put some things in water there is a force that can make them float. This force is called **buoyancy**. Buoyancy keeps boats afloat and also makes you float in a swimming pool.

Forces in your life!

Blow up a balloon and try to hold it under water in a large sink. Can you feel the buoyancy force pushing the balloon upwards?

When something goes into water it pushes some of the water out of the way. The water pushes back with an upward force. If the upward force is larger than the **weight** of the object, the object will float. If the upward force is smaller, the object will sink.

When a boat moves forwards there are lots of forces pushing and pulling it. The engine pushes the boat forwards. This force needs to be bigger than the **drag** of the water or the boat will not move.

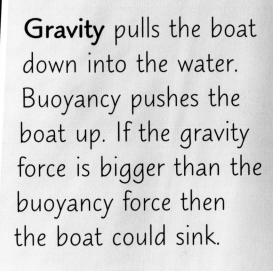

Gravity pulls the boat down into the water. Buoyancy pushes the boat up. If the gravity force is bigger than the buoyancy force then the boat could sink.

Lots of forces push and pull at a boat in the water!

Hitting and hammering

You can **exert** a lot of force on an object by hitting it with something else. If the force happens very quickly there is a large **impact**. In sport people use rackets, clubs, and bats to hit balls very quickly.

Hammers are tools that can help you hit something with a big force. The end of the hammer is heavy, which means the force is larger.

A collision is when one object hits another with a large force. The forces in collisions can do a lot of damage as the objects crash together. If two cars have a collision the people in the cars can be hurt because of the force of the collision.

This heavy ball is used to hit buildings and break them up.

Electricity and magnetism

A **magnet** makes a force that can push or pull against another magnet without even touching it! A magnet also pulls towards some types of metal, such as **iron** and **steel**. This is called a magnetic force.

Most fridge doors are made of steel. Magnets around the edge of the fridge pull towards the metal in the door. This magnetic force keeps the door shut.

You can stick things to the fridge using magnets. This art is held to the fridge because of the magnetic force between the magnet and the door.

Forces in electricity

Electricity is made by moving electric charges. These are small **particles** that can push and pull against each other.

When you rub a balloon against your jumper you rub some electric charges on to it. These charges can **exert** a pulling force on other things.

Forces in your life!

Try rubbing a balloon against your jumper and then see if you can make it stick to a wall.

Forces in the body

All of your **muscles** make forces in your body! In your arms there are two muscles that work as a pair. When you lift your hand up towards you the muscle on the top of your arm pulls it up. When you want to put your hand back down, the muscle under your arm has to pull it down.

Without forces we would not be able to bend our arms.

Other muscles in your body are like rings that can squeeze. Some of these are used to push food through your body. Others make the pupils in your eyes open and close.

Forces in your life!

Ask a friend to close their eyes tightly and put their hands over their eyes. Count to twenty and then ask them to open their eyes quickly. Look closely at the black pupils of their eyes when they do this. What happens?

Some of the forces in your body are very small, like the ones you use to open and close your eyes. Other forces are very big, like the ones you use in your **jaw** when you are breaking up your food to eat.

Facts about forces

Forces are measured in Newtons (N).

You can roughly work out the force of **gravity** on your body using this calculation:
Force of gravity on you = your **weight** (in kilograms) x 10

Even water coming out of a hose makes some **friction**, which can slow it down. Firefighters add a special **material** to the water they use to cut down the friction so that the water flows faster!

The force of gravity on Earth is six times bigger than the force of gravity on the Moon.

There is a type of rock called pumice stone that can sometimes float! It has so many air bubbles in it that it is **buoyant** on water. You may have some of this stone in your bathroom. It can be used to rub skin off your feet.

If you want to balance on a see-saw the forces pushing down on both sides have to be the same.

Find out more

You can find out more about science in everyday life by talking to your teacher or parents. Your local library will also have books that can help. You will find the answers to many of your questions in this book. If you want to know more, you can use other books and the Internet.

Books to read

Discovering Science: Energy, Rebecca Hunter
  (Raintree, 2003)
Science Answers: Forces and Motion, Chris Cooper
  (Heinemann Library, 2003)
Science Files: Forces and Motion, Steve Parker
  (Heinemann Library, 2004)

Using the Internet

Explore the Internet to find out more about forces. Try using a search engine such as www.yahooligans.com or www.internet4kids.com, and type in keywords such as "**buoyancy**", "**friction**", and "**gravity**".

Glossary

buoyancy force that pushes things up and keeps them afloat in water

drag force that slows things down when they move through air or liquid

electricity form of energy that can be used to make things work. Computers and televisions work using electricity.

exert when you exert a force on something you are pushing or pulling it

friction force that happens when two things rub together. Friction can slow things down or stop them from moving.

gravity force that pulls everything towards the centre of Earth

grip hold firmly

impact force that happens suddenly or quickly

iron type of metal that is magnetic and can also be made into a magnet

jaw large bone in the bottom of your mouth that holds your teeth

magnet special material that can stick to other magnets, or to some metals

mass amount of material something has in it

material something that objects are made from

muscles parts of the body that help us to move around

particles very tiny pieces. Everything all around you is made up of particles.

skid slip and slide smoothly over a surface

steel type of metal that is magnetic

surface top, or outside part of an object

weight how much material something has, and how much gravity pulls on it. We say heavy things weigh a lot and light things do not weigh very much.

Index

Titles in the *Science In Your Life* series include:

Hardback   1 184 443658 6

Hardback   1 844 43662 4

Hardback   1 844 43659 4

Hardback   1 844 43663 2

Hardback   1 844 43660 8

Hardback   1 844 43664 0

Hardback   1 844 43661 6

Find out about the other titles in this series on our website www.raintreepublishers.co.uk